P9-DME-667

# DISCARDING THE RAG DOLL

# DISCARDING

# THE RAG DOLL

**Written by**

## Kaytee Thrun

**Artist Contributors:**

Alberto Aprea
Johnny Perkins
Amy Kollar Anderson
Friederike Gröpler
Heather Dittmar

Paperback edition ISBN: 979-8-9859796-0-2
eBook edition ISBN: 979-8-9859796-1-9

Cover Art Credits:
Alberto Aprea - *Acrylic on canvas 2019 (front cover)*
Nathan James - *Photography 2022 (back cover)*

Copy Editing and Graphic Design by Marie Lee

Published by October City Press
1552 S. Route 59 #1193, Naperville IL 60564 USA
Media inquiries, bulk sales, and reproduction permission requests:
Jon Martin, *PR & Marketing Director* jm@kayteethrun.com

Acknowledgements and Inspirations

> *"Remember to thank those who inspire you."*
> *-Kaytee Thrun*

Alberto Aprea

**Friederike Gropler**

**Johnny Perkins**

**Jon Martin**

Amy Kollar Anderson

**Heather Dittmar**

## The Journey

Please open your heart
As locked away as it may be
Please enjoy all the syllables
As you are on your way
Into a world ripped apart
Where all your demons say
This is not the place
For you to forever stay
Stitch up that bleeding heart
Kick the door away
Jump into the rabbit hole
You will never be the same…

7/29/2022

## Author's Statement

My love affair with creating began as a child spending every afternoon in my parent's floral and antique shop. As the only daughter of artistic parents with few limitations, my eyes were always able to see the beauty and potential in even the strangest things. On one trip to an auction with my parents, we came home with a rickshaw, a wicker coffin, a king's sword and scepter, and a laboratory skeleton. Many days like that one fueled my sense of imagination and eccentricity.

Over time, my hands and mind have experimented with many forms of creativity that allow me to bring a feeling or an image to life through art that can be shared everyday with everyone around me. Having published multiple books with more on the horizon, the journey to combine words and images to master a "novel-in-poems" never ceases. Drawing from my past as a fine art fair jeweler, the desire to collaborate with other visual artists, photographers, and crafters is a form of hypnosis and it has me under its spell.

At this juncture of my life finding my own extraordinary side has been a journey and my stories are screaming to be told. It is with great hope that you may find a piece of my work that will inspire you to be who you are.

"Remember to thank those who inspire you."

# TABLE OF CONTENTS

- Reddest Wine
- Unsetting the Table
- Black Parasol
- Dead Bouquets
- Chased by Old Lovers
- Haunting Lovers
- The Raven
- Old Bookstores
- All My Photographs Tell
- Rare Works
- Not Born Out of Love
- White Dresses
- Letter to My Ex
- Scattering Music
- Restless Spirits
- Old Stories and Lies
- Seamstress
- Darling Vodka and Grenadine
- Stamps and Knitting Needles
- 35mm Photographs
- Obsidian
- Broken Glass Bruise
- Stitched on Heart

- The Honey of Poison
- Unbothered Dirt
- Reflections
- Masquerade
- Wicked
- The Spider
- Caged in Meaning
- Bohemian Trickster
- Disrobed
- Ashes and Sirens
- Autumn
- Haunted
- Been Bewitched
- Hades My Love
- Slayers
- Beneath Me
- Small Creatures
- Black Burnt Gate
- Dragon Bones
- The Vulture

- A Hundred Different Times
- Kisses on the Staircase
- The Catacombs
- Stained Glass
- Captivity
- No More Roses
- Cirque
- Where You Used to Live
- Needle and Thread
- Train Stops
- Wishing Well
- Ferris Wheel
- Incomplete Masterpieces
- Riding the Train Alone
- Remembering Crimson
- Wallpaper
- Apparitions
- The Owl
- Discarding
- Remember to Blink
- Stained Impressions
- Shameful Dark
- Metal Handcuffs on Concrete

- Clean the Attic
- My Colors, My Hues
- The Good Shelf
- Galaxy
- Blossoming
- Tulip Leaves
- Vanquish
- Tea Party
- Bewitched
- Shimmer
- Honeybees
- Spiral Staircase
- Memory Glass
- Storm Clouds
- Lost Luggage
- Pretty but Crazy
- Fearlessly
- Phoenix
- J 'adore la Danse
- Pages of Poison
- Bath Water
- Umbrellas on a Rock
- Pied-à-terre
- Rag Doll
- Raised Red Memories
- Black Bowes in Water
- Like Shards of Glass
- In Good Spirits
- Pied Piper
- Beautiful but Damaged
- Pocketworms
- Enchant Me
- #fearless

# DISCARDING
# THE RAG DOLL

# My Past Lovers

*Phyxiated by © Amy Kollar Anderson*
*Acrylic on canvas: 12" x 14" 2011 in private collection*

Reddest Wine

Each drop of my blood is a universe
Microscopic worlds spinning in red wine

My eyes get drunk on you in seconds
Drops bleed into your empty glass

Each sip taming the other in more ways
Clinking crystal makes hollow sounds

Like empty bones struck together
The melody of the cracking branches

You drink me deeply in intoxicated blood
Lips reddened off the glass rim shine wet

You seem to be the only one to notice...


2/13/2021

*Photography by Johnny Perkins*

## Unsetting the Table

My story has played out quite like the chaos of thunder
Taking handfuls of silverware and throwing them into the car
engine

Just to turn it on while it rattled and clanked viciously
Inside is the utter accustomed chaos, but from outside lulls

Rhythmic metallic drum beats that echo the storm rain
We fool ourselves into thinking it is nothing but music

Until the steam starts to hiss and the flatware burns chestnut
This machine was not designed to exist in extraordinary chaos

But it seems that I was...


10/30/2020

*Photography by Johnny Perkins*

Black Parasol

Nightmares or possibly fortuitous dreams each late sunset
Have me just slow pace strolling down an old boardwalk
Lace parasol twisting in my fingers and spinning in circles above
my cerebellum

Impossibly tiny warm raindrops speckle my shoes, but who counts
them all? Not me
This walk seemed necessary to move beyond and forward
Still hearing echoes though sometimes, don't lie, we still do

Each cut or bruise or unkind word showed us their demons
Trying to claw their way into our worlds through scratches and
vicious bites

Every sunrise to sundown stayed too long still haunts us
The exaggerated play acted out to finally secure back our hearts
was dramatic, but worthy

We once wanted to crush those dry broken hearts in our bare hands
for they held too much ache
But in the warmth of this downpour, the water is on my face and
cleansing me

Washing away the stench of you and the poison that always
dripped from your lips
For once in my life this flood is not tears, just raindrops escaping
through my spinning black parasol...

10/2/2020

Dead Bouquets

Flowers spilled from my lips, daisies and lilies, roses with thorns that cut me and made me bleed
They poured out as broken words that should have been spoken, but were not

You never brought me flowers, not once
You simply piled dead petals and leaves in my path for me to navigate around
On the other side was never beauty or love or life

So, do not speak words, speak in colors
The pinks of carnations, the whites of lily of the valley, the purples of hyacinth, and the deep deep red of the roses that bleed from my lips

The release of what cannot be spoken, not to you, not now
But someday, my lips will smile
And brilliant blooms will form and catch in my hands

A life without you, without thorns, with words and love
With the promise of someday being gifted a single flower to cherish and hold from blossom to death...

11/23/2019

*As If My Fingers Bleed Petals by Alberto Aprea*

*Photography by Johnny Perkins*

# Chased by Old Lovers

Saw Alice by the all the trash cans in a pale blue dress
Sweet charity she seeks in the mix of bad, spoiled, and rotten

Filth from clearly the source of the stench that invades her nostrils
Stains her dress brown and black and seemingly is just unfixable

She chased the hatters, as she was once mad for each
They all had several faces and even more masks painted red like
diablo

Chase her through the dark forest, no you will not
Chase her through the dirty city streets instead

Where trash and tragedy meet and the stains are less visible on the
blue
She can blend into the brickwork and hide until the garbage truck
rolls by luring...


8/19/2020

*Photography by Johnny Perkins*

## Haunting Lovers

Feeling rough fingertips make contact with my skin, but no one is there, you haunt me, who are you?
With my eyes tightly closed my body still knows of your touch somehow

Which one of my haunting dead lovers are you?

Those memories bleed into each other, but they are like the red petals of a flower
Meant to be picked and to inhale their intoxicating scent and then tossed to the ground where they shrivel and die

In some ways, all my lovers have died, some swiftly with words and others harshly with actions that speak old volumes on shelves

Your time has passed, why are you here?
My longing is to love in extraordinary chaos

Many forgotten faces under masks and not one part of me cares to know which one of my haunting dead lovers are you…

2/28/2020

The Raven

My locks were long
They flowed out in waves and engulfed you
Thinking you were blissfully charmed
The day you walked into my life, my world
Your raven with dark dark hair

You brought me into your lair
Tricking myself in control all along
My friend, my lover, my life, my months and years
Those days shall always sit in heaven in my memories

Although like a dark bird, you swooped in and attacked
My hair knotted, my hands scratched and scraped
My world left bleeding

Wishing you had stayed
Wishing you would leave
Learning to love and stretching my black wings out to reach to
you, alas
You were too far gone away already

You left me alone, perched, broken
A damaged bird of prey

We both were unable to fly, unable to keep loving
Only able to exist apart...


12/1/2019

*Photography by Johnny Perkins*

## Old Bookstores

You seduced me in the bookstore
As my fingers ran across the spines of prose
You pushed me up against a bookcase
Palms on either side of my face and kissed me hard

Blushing, as if others were watching
Knowing that you wanted me, knowing that you needed me
And you knew of course my cells and tears felt the same

You read novels of me, word by word
Memorized my favorite quotes and let them spill from your lips in
such vivid color

You seduced others, but I never could, as my heart cannot break
for two people at once

Simply scattered into broken syllables
Unspoken and damaged, scars from sharp words that are carried to
this day
Old words grew stale like first editions stacked on a shelf,
forgotten, and covered in dust

But my fingers still run the spines of books
Daydreaming of what they hold inside
Is it love? Is it hate? Betrayal? Lust? Fantasy?

My curiosity keeps me going back to the shelves
Looking for that story that wants and needs to be read…

12/10/2019

*Demons Hide in The Prose by Alberto Aprea*

All My Photographs Tell

Digging through the old boxes in my attic with dust in my nose
Looking for all the forgotten memories buried and taped up

Finding old photographs where it is amazing to see yourself
There next to him and not even recognize that love used to live
there

Why some of us save but are rare to view them if ever is unknown
While others burn their film to ashes or toss them all back

Before picking this box up, my decision had been made
Each photograph is a story of mine whispering to be spoken...


12/6/2020

*Photography by Johnny Perkins*

Rare Works


Hanging snowflakes outside my window and staring so long,
thinking that they were real
Outside the world was simply a picture you painted with colors
that began to run, as my eyes fixated on the images

How longing to see this picture as truth, but it never will be
Forced to face that none of this was ever as beautiful

The brush strokes were not as smooth, the colors uneven
The snowflakes hanging on strings like marionettes and me as your
puppet also

Pushing aside the painting, the strings, the facade
Focusing on the world as it is
Rougher, brighter, scarier, my eyes squinting

But if nothing else, it is real to finally accept that even the most
incredible works of art can be faked

The true test of anything great is time...


12/14/2019

*Photography by Johnny Perkins*

## Not Born Out of Love

Secrets in bedsheets and nighttime whispers and the lack thereof of
anything to prohibit the next great life
Whether we ever spoke of it or not, our actions spoke rare first
edition novels of it, volumes, and kisses

Create a demon or an angel or one who was just beautiful but a
little dark inside, half you, half me

But that, oh that, that never came true, though we did try
inventively for many trips around the sun and back

Never since then did that repeat, never tried so hard, never wanted
enough, longing sets in that seeps into your bones

They ache as the journey goes on making treasure out of trash and
gold out of tin foil and always seeking my soul

And that life never came to us, just reared its beautiful yet tragic
head, as we made sense of the senseless happening

You conquered me in many ways, but left scars so deep they are
inside, and no amount of hand stitches could reach and repair the
pieces of me still parted...


2/4/2020

## White Dresses

As little girls in white dresses, we enact weddings in our backyards by gathering flowers from the bushes and marrying our friends

Our fingers were grass-stained and mom's make-up sparkling on our faces overdone, lipstick that would smear over play time and a lifetime too

Growing in age, resigning myself to being alone for all my trips around the sun
It was not until we met that the mere idea of it resonated

You enchanted me, seduced me sure, danced with me, but before the dress, you loved me legitimately

My foolishness believing you were the one that got away, but you were not lost, you were meant to go and did go
We were meant to love then and only then, that many suns, you were meant to leave me, I was meant to break apart

But scars remain deep, scars that are all but healed now, but bled me once

Stained my white dress with red spots and left questions and spaces where feelings used to live
Ripped small tears in the sheer fabric where sense used to be found

By little girls who want to feel connected in shimmering grass-stained fabric stolen from my mom's closet

For when we were small, we all dreamed to be her and ended up becoming her after the secrets in the darkness peaked out...

2/1/2020

*Witnesses in the Yard by Alberto Aprea*

## Letter to My Ex

We worked hard to make ends meet and saw each other every hour
of every day of every month
At first the intoxication of being together was indescribable and
did feed our souls and empty hearts

Some days we would sleep in, some days it would rain

These types of days fed me to stay and for years, having to admit,
you were wonderful to me, but my fear never rested and your
desire to wander did not either

When you eventually did wander and kept coming around telling
me everything would be alright, but it never was alright, was it?
And when you finally disappeared, my soul searched for you for
years in the face of every person touched or kissed

Was it love or something else?
It was something else
But eventually the fog cleared and showed the world a side of me
too scared to show you

In the end, my love was given in great abundance and my hope is
that once in a while, gazing out the window you can still think, she
was an unbreakable kind of girl…

1/31/2020

## Scattering Music

My fingers grasp the peeling wood railing on the balcony
Chilled wind blows my hair into my eyes and of course, it annoys
me

My hands tick to keep brushing it away in tempered anxiety
Waiting for you to come home is like feeling you left me each day

Dried up leaves rustle along the sidewalk in symphony
Like an army of bugs marching in sync legs click to the ground

Ghosts of my memories of us pass by in the wet fog to their music
Reminding me that most of our past is actually haunted

And you never come home as my fingers freeze to the railing
Slivers in my hand from the chipping paint, but still waiting

Until that stopped and my frozen fingers, bent and broken
Unclenched and shook the last chip of you off my skin forgotten

Years passed on that balcony waiting for foretold futures
Daydreams that evolved into all of my nightmares

That unlike your ghosts lost perilously in the fog
All my bad memories spirited away on rustling leaf wings...

1/22/2021

*Photography by Johnny Perkins*

Restless Spirits

The lattice of the metal frame gate of the cemetery was locked for
the night
Our fingers gripped the bars like claws as we peered inside and
watched the ghosts float from grave to grave

They were lost, as were we
They had lost the ability to speak, and we had no words left to say
to each other

Life and death and death of love

While we could not enter the cemetery, but just peer through and
look as if we could walk amongst the headstones reading the faded
names of the dead

Mingling with the spirits in the hopes of regaining a voice, but we
could not
We simply watched them as they eventually retreated to the safety
of their own graves
Clawing deep into the dirt with their boney fingers

Restless and still believing they were alive
Just as we believed our love still took in breath after breath until
suffocating…

11/9/2019

## Old Stories and Lies

All those things that take more than time to get past
Those little idiosyncrasies that you do each day that stick in my
memory like glued pages
Your tone of voice lingers, still hearing the echo of the quite
beautiful you spoke with an endearing melody

After you decided to betray me, those words spoken were rarely
painless and usually quite sharp

It is those things whether miniscule or enormous that tickle in the
back of my throat when speaking of you
Soft words turned to harsh tones after we lied and laughed about
whether or not you have a heart

In the end you do have one, though likely a deeper shade of red
beating slower these years than mine

Still sometimes my thoughts of you are dark as well, but now my
heart is bright and beating and not littered with cobwebs from your
old stories and lies...

4/11/2020

\

Seamstress

Hanging on to a long single thread that stretched out day after day,
month after month, year after year
It wrapped tightly around my fingertips and over time it dug in
deeply

But never letting loose of that thread of hope that someday you
would come back to me
Never letting go, until one day my hand slipped free, and it
fluttered away, but you would never fully leave me

The deep scars on my fingertips where the thread made me bleed
would remain
But we were never meant to be tied, to be bound by that thread, to
be woven close together

The logical part of me knows now and has known for years that we
had to untie, that we had to part, that you had to unravel and set me
free…

12/3/2019

*Photography by Johnny Perkins*

## Darling Vodka and Grenadine

Several years ago the man that sat at my table for dinner simply
disappeared
He took the life that breathed in him and said farewell in short
words

In distance, one can only do so very little but call to the rafters for
some help and relief
But it came far too late, as the tresses of his brown hair hit the hard
concrete

Never having auditioned nor wanted to be a part of this theater of
death
But you forced me to play a part and it ran on for miles

As your head is heavy and full of darling vodka and grenadine, you
sleep
Leaving me with a burden never deserved and finally now laying
down the boulder of your memory and traveling on...

7/1/2020

*Photography by Johnny Perkins*

Stamps and Knitting Needles

At first meeting, you wove me the story of your life
Yarn by yarn you told me of your conquests
The monsters you have slayed and maidens you have saved
The foreign lands and passports with many stamps
Craving that adventure, drawn to the smoke bellowing from your
nose

But those pieces of yarn began to fray, one by one
There were no conquests, not now not ever
There was no glory, not now not ever
There were no stamps on a passport

There was only a lifetime of frayed yarns, dropped stitches, and
piles and piles of weave on the floor
The life of a gypsy you wove from lie to treacherous lie
Once liking how you called the world vicious

Now stitches just drop to the floor and never having learned to
knit, sweeping the yarn into a messy tied pile, the twisted story of
what your life truly wove

My passport clutched in my fingertips with much room for stamps
you will never dry ink from…


11/14/2019

## 35mm Photographs

A shaky blurred image is all you ever were, captured in a
photograph
Standing behind you, as my figure always seemed to be

There was never a smile on your face, as on mine
Caught living in an illusion with a figment
Displaced and foreign these images seem to me now

If there ever was joy, it is not remembered
Only the bitter tears of your failure and falsities

One trip around the sun was enough with you
One season of masquerading was all of you
One minute of peace now is mine

Each picture without you in it is breathtaking
As my heart is recovered and moved on to new photographs where
my smile is authentic

You still never smile…


12/27/2019

Obsidian

The world is afloat on a sea of molten lava, shifting tectonic plates
tock us back and forth sometimes
If you think of things in life that should run miles of shivers up our
spines, it should be that burning sea or the like

But it is not, for that which terrifies us most is the cracking,
crashing, implosion of our hearts and every minute that was truly
not impactful

Should not we then focus on that sea, navigating it safely, for love
should never bite so hard, it should be soft and full of a million
yeses and tons of always

Choose to seek it, choose to not fear it, you are on the surface, for
it is not a flame, it cannot kill you, it can only bruise you until you
heal, and we always heal...

2/3/2020

*Photography by Johnny Perkins*

Broken Glass Bruise

Your eyes like marbles as you hold me close, my past lovers
My heart shatters like it's made of glass inside my chest

We had to love painfully hard and we had to let go when we did
Joined through the red streaks from shards where our hearts used
to be

In time they all will be plucked out and put back together with glue
Our hearts may be patchwork now, but we can still beat too

Push back the memories of when we loved each other viciously
Mending the cracks before they turn into more endings

Filling our pockets with glue to still use with our fingertips cut
from each cut broken glass bruise...


10/14/2020

*Photography by Johnny Perkins*
*Art Rag Doll by Heather Dittmar*

Stitched on Heart

Clock ticks moments of lost consciousness
Bleeding eternally from this chest wound
Where you ripped right through me

Stuck here stuffing it full of cotton fluff
Keeping my blood inside was just enough
Then every part of me would not dry up

Perhaps in a hundred years or so
Stitches my fingers weave will thread it up or no
Sewing the misshape of a broken heart

Delicately over the cotton sewn
Hiding the missing beating muscle below bone
Wondering if anyone will ever know...


7/11/2021

# My Instigators

*What the Dormouse Said by © Amy Kollar Anderson*
*Acrylic on canvas: 10" x 16" 2012 in private collection*

## The Honey of Poison

Sing lovely to me, as your words sound just like honey
Drowning me with the lyrical wisdom of your sins

Your scent of menthol and bad memories wisps into me
But no matter the struggle, the bees spinning entice me in

Drinking from the chalice of your lies, my lips burning
Not realizing the effects until it was too late to turn around

My broken and longing smile downturned and fiery red
Your bee sting came too late for me to run and hide

The pests disguise in masks just outside...


10/6/2020

*Photography by Johnny Perkins*

Unbothered Dirt

With bare feet on the earth after ditching those high heels
One single victory from trading spiked tongues with red fiends

Turns out the devil was short and therefore my life shrank too
Until sinking so low to dig in dirt with my claws to uncover

The true nature of danger in his tornado of lies, so his punishment
was utter humiliation, as diablo prizes pride

In the public square so meticulously crafted this exercise of defeat
In private, no never

Tempt me again as even withered, it appears my fight is quite
orchestrated like a symphony of fingers playing music dirt under
nails

Giving up appears to be something never learned and that my soles
cherish as they take a step through unbothered dirt...


11/8/2020

*Photography by Johnny Perkins*

## Reflections

Spending my life sold in the mirror, focused on being enough or trying to just fake it
Never having whatever that mix of paint and love and confidence was, it eluded me

Chasing each dream, intoxicated by them, while all along, it was me they each chased and consumed
Cell by cell and bit of bone, each strand of hair and fingertip and tendon

Cannot act like my life is lived without mirrors, without being able to see my face beneath the paint and stain
Their faces too for that matter, just the damned ghost reflections that light up with hot breath on them

The looking glass, she always reflects me so strong and confident in the eyes, it is my favorite reflection
On her face is where comfort lives, where anyone can trick me beautiful...

4/27/2020

## Masquerade

All of you, my mistakes and instigators, my liars and devils, and my slow dance poisoners
You are all the same person hiding under different masks in seasons and ballrooms having lived through

Loving you all the same though, giving my heart still beating in my hands, and watching you twist and warp it
Taking it back all that was left was something damaged and with no remedy or cure

Then to inevitably repeat, your face in a mask, another you but just another you, nothing ever more
With you there to break me again, my heart in such worse shape this time, but time again

She peeks out with hesitation and wants me to ask someone to spin her gracefully again
That is why the mask chase calls to me in the hopes this masquerade ball ends with me learning to dance...


4/26/2020

*We Still See You by Alberto Aprea*

*Photography by Johnny Perkins*

Wicked


We stomped on grapes and drank glasses full of deep roses
My thoughts spun about me like satin ribbons entangling

While the earth beneath me shuddered with each step
You like a lion, led me straight into your still darkness
The universe spun about me with whipping wind

Unable to discern fantasy from non-fiction from horror theme
playing out here
You tell me "You are beautiful when you are crying" and my lips
sound out no
Your lips hit mine with a bang and my eyes sink into the darkness
swelling

Awakening with my exposed bones gripping my ruby slippers,
silently escaping as the sun peaked, you are asleep
Disappearing back into the forest, as this path was yours to weather
and mine to burden now

The tornado of my life began with your single poisonous unwanted
breath...


9/8/2020

*Photography by Johnny Perkins*

The Spider

The ether of the world is where all your lies are exposed
And searching within, finding all that was needed to see
The results of your actions, the punishment, the finality

When the spider comes for you in your web of lies
It will wrap you in a cocoon and slowly suck out your liquified
insides
You are never safe from that spider
He will always come for you

Everything lives forever they say
But you my friend will not live forever, and your legacy will be
sorrow and shame

But the spider does not care
She will devour you anyway
Bit by tiny bit
Finger by toe by eyeball

She will taste every single bit of you with her fangs until there is
nothing left of you, but a shell
A cold empty cocoon that the wind will suck up and blow away, as
the spider finishes with you…

11/14/2019

## Caged in Meaning

Deep in the basement of our multi-unit, sat wire cage storage lockers within a dark maze of hallways
It was where people kept holiday decorations and lights, family heirlooms, and cobwebs

It was where we ended up one night on the hard and dirty floor, though not remembering how or why
In earlier days with you, moments like this were exciting and adventurous

On this night, it was simply the filth on my bare skin, the spiders crawling across webs, the single lightbulb hanging from the ceiling, and the total blackness of your eyes

This would not be our last adventure though, as you locked me in one of those cages and you had the only key
Periodically, you would let me out, but never come in

I would reach out my hand, but it would not be taken
I would reach out my heart, but it would be rejected

On days alone, simply wrapping my fingers through the wire mesh and watch the spiders dance from threads
Squinting to see if the dark silhouette in the corner was you coming to save me or use me or set me free

Or is it the shadow of an antique locked in another cage waiting for purpose?
As my shell sits waiting for my purpose again…

12/10/2019

*Photography by Johnny Perkins*

## Bohemian Trickster

No fortune teller could have foretold this gypsy train stop
That my feet stepped off on as the steam hissed and popped

Loathe the station seemed vivid and the bricks were quite rough
But wicked brews and fake jewels litter my cobblestone shoes

Had my eyes not been fancied by your gypsy words dancing
Entranced by the rumble of the train leaving me here frantic

Running for a train car not traveled by tricksters not chanced it
My fingertips clutching the pole as the hiss steams right past you...


11/9/2020

*Deceptively Dead Time Teases the Queen by Alberto Aprea*

Disrobed

Five garments in the closet, years of pain, and an old typewriter is all you ever had
Therefore, stripping the clothes off my back
The clock on the wall ticking time backwards

This world of ours may be another planet's hell, they say
And no matter what, my dreams and nightmares would just go on for miles
My back would be bare
Exposed to the raw elements of rain, dirt, and the sharp wind that cuts me

And your closet would be full, but never your heart
You would rip it out and hand it to me, black and dead
In my hands it would crumble like ashes
Spill through my fingertips to the ground

For it was not for me ever
Darkness claimed it long ago with cold boney fingers that took each molecule of your soul, turning it black and quite rotten…

12/27/2019

*My Key is Missing by Alberto Aprea*

Ashes and Sirens

On this planet there are rocks and lakes and there are mountains
and immense trees
There is water to give life and there are flames to take it all rushed
away

Daydreaming of you in the forest and you are green and alive and
everything glorious
Falling to your leaves that drip with dew and running my fingers
down your branches
You are life, my life, but life is an illusion of colors
Cool shades that turn warm

The sun creeps down below the horizon and the temperature rises
and rises, and the trees begin to burn
Their life melts and twists into unrecognizable shapes of black and
darkness and fear

You smirk as the flames lap around you
Your brilliant leaves turn crisp brown and expose all that is real
and true

Left is just you, naked, withered branches twisted into your
skeleton

Still in this moment while watching you burn, you try to call to me
like a siren
But no, it is time to crave water, to crave life and blues and greens

You reach a brittle hand out to me in one last effort to pull me into
you
But instead remaining in color, in life and watching as you slowly
break apart and blow away
Nothing but ash and bad memories

The wind falls me back with eyes closed
Caught with gentle hands in the water that has come for me
Becoming my own siren, to serenade me home
My voice, my voice, my voice
Echoes in the forest, tumbles the rocks
Puts out the flames and saves me...


9/17/2019

*Photography by Johnny Perkins*

Autumn


While not becoming lovers with the devil on purpose, for soon I found myself in his bed
His viciousness in every way was of legend, and he cut open my veins just to watch me bleed
Charm, wit, and twisted ways exuded from like sweat and poisoned me

It was a hard spell to break, but it happened and my sewed up bloodied heart with black yarn left purposefully

Not every lesson to learn is clear or comfortable or kind, as this was not any of those
Autumn is the leaving, what happens when those bent trees release orange and yellow leaves
And prepare for a time of darkness and death

But burnt into my skin is the scar from the yarn holding in my full red beating heart no longer cursed...


4/13/2020

*Photography by D B Lee*

Haunted

Daydreaming for dreams, wishes for the future, just something real is all we seek
Asking for guidance, no direction, for hope, and the dark angel answered me instead

In his delicious ways, he sent me his demons, each one much worse than the last, until you
Fearlessly you used words as weapons and love as a knife, you stained my soul blood red

Begging for redemption, he chased his darkness away, you listened, and you left
The house could crumble, the world could end, and still you creep from the burning rubble

But foolish no more, each one only stole a piece of my heart, there is just enough left
To never trick me beautiful, twist my words, or make me feel less than just haunted again…

5/14/2020

Been Bewitched


Looking at me, you knew words swarmed in my head like bees
preparing to strike viciously as they must do
Armed with proof of your continued snake tongue of lies

Consuming me, bit by bit with your intoxicating stare
Shattering the glass that cocooned me in safety
Your tongue licks the red that drips hot down my face
Your whispered words, instructions, rules
The heart cannot win, it always has won

Until my blood pools and boils
Burning my skin with your torturous eyes
The words of truth leak out and bleed onto your palms
Allowing me to see the true you behind the mask

You are bewitched in disbelief as my leaving is unburdened
You are not the devil
You do not hold that power

For I would rather spend a thousand nights alone
Then spend one more night in your desolation...


9/16/2019

## Hades My Love

Maybe we each have to go to underworld once in our lives and pay the gondolier in pennies on the river Styx
Just to be rebreathed with the ability to decide who we want to be the next chance around
Maybe some of us visit there twice or even more

The claws of the journey scratch beneath our feet all the time, tempting to drag us backwards into bad memories

Are those burning electric butterflies in our stomachs? Is it love or betrayal or lust this time?
Will the burns on the palms of our hands from the journeys stop stinging?

Left to dust, pebbles, specs of sand, ashes, a few pennies, and a longing we all burden…


4/29/2020

*Photography by D B Lee*

Slayers

Someone has to be the one to travel one more level into the deeper blackness and darkness
To seek out the demons and snakes that lurk within it that hunt for the weakest of us

What cursed thing was committed in a past life that gifts me this awful journey?
Year after gut-stabbing year of peeling the masks off devils and revealing no skin beneath

Once their bloodied faces are shown, their absolute strength and endless sway recedes
And my red fingers can claw me out of the dark again and at the surface it blinds me

But it is never for long, as the sun will still set no matter how much we pray or we don't
And some of us, give up all of ourselves, to hunt the ones who will and have killed so many unremembered faces...


7/20/2020

*Photography by Johnny Perkins*

Beneath Me

Within every relationship's ending we die just a tiny bit
Then all those dead pieces just chip off and scattered like broken
glass on the floor
A million tiny shards that make your feet bleed

Our old shell may break away, but beneath it is much more alive
than you can remember being
That part of us inside, that soul that lives just beneath the surface
of the skin survives
She hid within the layer of me

That devil he tries to steal her, but cannot because he holds no
blade and cannot puncture the skin, he tries with a kiss

She is still there, that other me, between arteries and veins, beneath
muscle and tendons, she survived
For today, do not die a little, live a little, and a little more
tomorrow, and a little more after that

To chip away it all off and be fresh like green grass and new like
Spring's birth
Just to get a glimpse of this world that we had since forgotten…


1/31/2020

*Photography by Johnny Perkins*

## Small Creatures

My bedsheets have holes in them from all the broken dreams
That creep slowly into my nights, up my leg and into my head

Some are etched deep and some woken with sweat
Haunting me either way when my greens peel open

Pushing them away for the glass is half full in my hand
Pouring it over my head to cool the remains of my thoughts

You can catch me when deep in the solitude of sleep
In the light of day, you are chased away like rats with a flute

Serenading your exit with screeches, small legs, and contaminated
wisdom...


10/25/2020

## Black Burnt Gate

Several have been inside of me, but only a few reached my beating heart, as most fake loved and wanted me and left me broken on the way out

Always falling for it, as my weakness is love and the warmth of the wrap, but you stain the bed ice cold each time that you leave me

You lulled me into a sense of deep nothingness without expectations with those wicked and warned deceptive dark eyes you have

Slowly guiding me by hand through the rusty gates of your hell, but the demons they wanted just you and thanked me for bringing you

They cleared the poison of you from my brain left you behind with the tornados of black snakes and lakes of red-eyed toads swirling

Letting you attempt to coax them out to play, but their fangs just laugh at you with your witchery of words and vile tongue still lying

There are things in the ether more dark and quite lovelier than you and one just opened the gate with burnt hands as my feet pass right through...

10/18/2020

*Photography by Johnny Perkins*

Dragon Bones

Was caught up in the wind of you
Chasing the dragon of what was always wanted
To have love, to love with every tepid breath

Caught when younger for inches or moments
Microseconds of time until losing grip
Chasing for years, each kind voice, each sweet whisper
Finding it in empty shells with no souls and burns from the
dragon's breath on their shoulders

Until realizing it cannot be caught, not in this lifetime
My reach has shortened, chase slowed, the long black burnt claws
of the dragon scar my skin

Stinging, the flames lap up to my face, engulfing me, burning the
shell of me that now shows to contain, a crushing skeleton starved
to death, no heart, no spine

No soul left grieving...


1/16/2020

*Photography by Johnny Perkins*

The Vulture

Picking at my dying carcass you were for nearly a year after you
had left
You made empty promises that you would return, but each night,
the bed stayed cold

In my foolishness and my youth, believing your words
How the young mind whispers such sweet words in your head
spinning out the badness

You just continued to pick away at my ridged bones as you needed
me and the death in me allowed it
With love and fear, and fear of love in me

Until one day, you were just gone
Fooling myself with logic, but it was just foolish words

You left the broken remnants of my soul behind
No stitches in the world could put all of me back together
It would take pinching one stitch at a time, year after year leaving
thick red forever scars

As they healed slowly over time, the rest of the vultures circled
overhead waiting for me…

11/8/2019

# My Ghosts

*Wanderland by © Amy Kollar Anderson*
*Acrylic on canvas: 18" x 36" 2012 in private collection*

A Hundred Different Times

It was we who dated a hundred different times
With different faces that all eventually became yours

Many days that became many years
Of your touch, your lips, your syllables that consumed me

New faces bewitched to be you
New names mistaken with yours

All because for my whole life, love came too fast
Giving my soul to you in every lifetime
Letting you bleed me dry each time

Until empty and hollow waiting to be
Whole, complete, reborn
Without the sins caused me
Reading the names on the street signs
The letters move to form your name

A lifetime we passed between a hundred different times…

9/14/2019

*Photography by Johnny Perkins*

## Kisses on the Staircase

Having you my lover pitch curious passions to see which way
My cheeks may swell red or shall drink in the poison of you

Lingering kisses led to some tumbling falls on the staircase
As my heart went down step by step until it lands to burst open

Letting year after year pass with my fingers left scarred reaching
Trying to claw my way back up one by one with my heart gripped

But time ticked to reach the top, my chest open and breathing
swells
Gone, your ghost scents the room with musk and a foggy intention

To linger too long and curse hundreds of chances to stitch up the
damage
My fingers are pin cushions for so many reasons it is savage

So left somewhat rough and jagged with rocks in my backpack
At the top of the stairs tempted by my new curious passions...


1/21/2021

*Photography by Johnny Perkins*

The Catacombs

There is still blood in the catacombs no matter how many hundreds
of years pass
Deep and cold below the city where fingertips cannot help but
resist touching

One bone
One human skull
Because we never would have the chance again to

Quiet as nighttime in winter, but these are not men of snow

Skeletons and bones
Stacked thoughtfully creating artwork of the death

Closer to hell this deep is frightening yet exciting
Do their ghosts linger near the living?

What must each of their dreams have been long long ago?
Inside those yellowing skulls designed in a row

Did they paint beautiful stories of the future until all the colors ran
from tears?

The haunting beauty of the stolen faces of thousands
Peering back at onlookers seeking a true understanding of the
bridge between life and death...


10/8/2020

*Before My Wings Burnt by Alberto Aprea*

## Stained Glass

Dreaming in a field of flowers, soft silky yellows and hazy mint
greens
The wind barely blows but knows so much about me still
My eyes open wide and lip's part to let out all that is bottled up in
my beating heart and lungs

Butterflies escape my mouth and encircle about me, some landing
on my skin
Each wing a wonderful dream or a horrifying nightmare
Every word my lips hoped to speak flies on their soft colored
stained-glass frame, escaping into the world

You never were strong enough nor gentle enough to catch my
wings as they beat
But you were the love of my life then and only then
My soul would chase those butterflies in that field for years

Catching one in my shaking fingers, it would turn brown and dead
and crumble into the wind
Almost all have flown away or died since that time then
But still feeling one rustling inside my stomach, so desperate to be
freed

And someday maybe someway maybe, when breathing this one
and catch it in my hands, bent and tired
It will thrive and be colored again, not just stained brown from the
stench of time escaping…

1/26/2020

*Photography by Johnny Perkins*

Captivity

My old love, you captured me like an elusive creature deep in the jungle
You put me in captivity, but the closeness was worth every kept second there

Chronically each moment in my memories, a million photographs of your face, the taste of your lips, the smell of your skin

When you set me free to roam, my fingertips would run down your rough skin, scratch the stubble on your face
The illusion of losing time inside your dark eyes

But in later years, you would leave me captive, isolate me from my closest, the truth of the loneliness would set in
A thousand years spent waiting for you, but you had left me

If a soul is the being of happiness, the figure the lives just beneath our skin, that can be touched with a blade or a kiss
My soul met yours and would be forever encircled with mine, over miles of time

But there can be more souls to touch, and my hands will seek out parts of you in others, to cobble together that who is next to love...

1/20/2020

*Photography by Johnny Perkins*

No More Roses

The first time realizing my bleeding beating was gone from your
heart was when the roses stopped coming
You always brought me single roses, but no more

You wore your heart on your sleeve and handed to me red on a
vine or so my damaged heart wanted to believe
Our love our love seemed binding and strong
But dwindled still

As the sweet scent of flowers died and was replaced by the stink of
love's death in you...

6/24/2014 revised 8/23/2020

*Photography by Johnny Perkins*

Cirque

Years passed as dreams of you returning waned
Foolish dreams that made for restless nights and sleep deprived
days

Your demon taunted me well and kept dragging me along
Despite how hard the struggle to break away
Your fingernails dug deeply into my arm
You did not want me, but you wanted to keep me

But your hands grew ever tired, and your grasp slipped
Being free was everything, but scared to run too far
From this show we had become so good at dancing
Waiting backstage, an understudy, for too long
Hoping the you my heart loved would return
But never should that pass

Just time, endless time, and days that eventually brightened and
made me wander off, leaving this circus stage
Let the clowns and the contortionists have it
Let the tent collapse and the crowd disperse
For this show is over and has been

Been done waiting in the wings and needing to accept it
Putting all eyes on me in the center of the ring just like a
sideshow...

1/7/2020

## Where You Used to Live

Some part of my brain deep within the grey matter, buried beneath webs of blood vessels, you live still
That part you inhabit, though years have passed, you never left completely

You tinker with the electricity in there and make me question logic and life
Have I truly loved or just been a prisoner of loving?
Have I been broken and healed or just broken?

But you will exit my cerebellum somehow with words or another's love or a medical instrument
Picking at you like a scab because no one belongs that far in my mind, least of all you, any of you

That space will fill up with flower buds and butterfly cocoons and let them birth
As they escape on their own when mature, flowers from my lips, beautiful things

My grey matter finally free of you and something much prettier growing in the place where you used to live...


2/6/2020

*Photography by Johnny Perkins*

*Photography by Johnny Perkins*
*Art Rag Doll by Heather Dittmar*

Needle and Thread

You had no coins at all in empty pockets
But you seemed to love me enough anyways

You hand sewn a red heart-shaped pillow
With uneven cut stitches and broken threads

You handed me your crooked heart that day
It was curated and loved until it wasn't

You left too many open dropped stitches
Eventually the stuffing all just fell out

You watched it spill onto the floor from my hands
Never even picking up a needle to sew us back together

Still have that pillow in a drawer somewhere
Collecting dust and smiles from only old good memories...


9/25/2020

*Photography by Johnny Perkins*

Train Stops

Do you think it was my choice to ride this broken train?
Staring glass-eyed out the window as the earth flies quite swiftly
by

My luggage is all unpacked, new things and old ones too, some
taped or glued
There are no stops on this train, it just rides the rails for weeks and
days

You opened this silver sliding door for me and shoved me into this
life
You must deal with whatever demons come through the dark door
too

They seem to still haunt me in the angry faces of all my past lovers
For already this train has made stops at the gates where the devils
all live

But never underestimate me, that would be fun, despite this trip,
my soul thrives
My hands have clutched the gate, my fingerprints burned, never
having had belonged there...


8/3/2020

## Wishing Well

Still the sensation of your hair twisted between my fingers
Strands of deep brown stain my skin like dye
Warm breath on my face, lips that touch to taunt and to tease me
My smile larger than life and immeasurably authentic

This space here, two inches from your face is where to stay
Engulfed in your oxygen, soft soft words, and the curve of your
lips as you snicker at me

But this twelve-by-twelve world never lasts, it dissipates
My hands tingle as your frame melts from between them
Vanishing, souls of you, empty dead air, sick butterflies, and
realizing all alone is where we end up most days

Tossing promises into the wishing well like coins
Wondering if the water is filled with your poison
Each wish significant and an eternity of fool-hearted waiting...


1/12/2020

*Drink Me, Devour Me by Alberto Aprea*

*Photography by Johnny Perkins*

Ferris Wheel

High atop the city in the glass Ferris wheel
From all directions we could see the fog covered peaks of the
mountains, the soft rippling water of the sound, and the checkboard
of buildings below

It was as high as we would ever be
As soon we would crash and fall

But in that moment, peering through the glass
With endless opportunities that lies before us
Feeling so much promise and so much hope

But then looking down
Through the glass floor
Seeing the tops of buildings caked with dirt and leaves
The reality that we would come down too

We would always crash and fall
We would always crash and burn
We would always end up at the bottom of the Ferris wheel
With the gears stuck, unable to go up, unable to get out, stagnant

Stuck in the same spot in the glass cage
Peering up and possibilities…


11/19/2019

*Photography by Johnny Perkins*

## Incomplete Masterpieces

Building up rocks into broken statues is a cautionary tale
Molded to perfection no, but too imperfect for me to see

Sculpting the crooked image of the one that got away
The one that left hard and left wrong and left open scars, raised red
scars that never healed completely

That is the problem when you build someone up high
Every single person for the rest of your life, you compare to a
falsity crafted in your memories

Statues will never be anything more than clay built by hands that
have imperfections and create imperfect things and that is the
blissful ignorance of love…

10/25/2019

*Photography by Johnny Perkins*

Riding the Train Alone


Dreaming always in full rich color, like that haunting old movie
'What Dreams May Come'
A field of oil paint covered flowers, royal blues, fiery reds
You dream in black and white, one dimensional, no depth, no
creativity, none at all
No thought even if a better ever was there

You never could see me behind your blackened sunglasses
Hiding the heavy bags sinking under your eyes, could you?
Or maybe that hid that tick you would do
Each time you spit superficial lies from your mouth into my
outstretched open hands

And now you wonder if I truly do hate you that much
Well the truth does not lie
And she does not know how to hate you, because she does not
even know who you are

You are a stranger on a train she once took…


5/12/2020

*Photography by Johnny Perkins*

Remembering Crimson

The reddest of leaves, like blood covered palms, dripped overhead as we stepped silently through the forest
As in so many ways of us, you were many steps ahead, letting me fall far far behind
Trying so hard to enjoy each footprint in the dirt, each scrape of a branch, each uneven rock, I did

But wishing you stood beside me to enjoy it too, but you were on your own journey
As usual, that path you walk, does not include me, and for once and that is fine with me

My road has red leaves and snowflakes and flowers and suns, but all yours will ever have is the fog and the grim dark rain and sadness

We can always say one got away, but in this instance, you were thrown away hard
Exposed your story thread of success and achievement, but the red leaves still die when they hit you, but it is better than the red red blood of a broken heart...


2/16/2020

Wallpaper

The walls were roses
Hundreds or thousands of them
Pinkest pink, soft blood red, intoxicating purple
Each bud representing a moment in my life

They began to dance, and they began to move, float
They swirled about me, all the living and even the dead roses
and broken memories
Petals dropped and covered the ground in a wall of roses
movement

Scents that still haunt me when smelling them
Colors that still stain my fingertips blush
To have had so many moments wonderful
To feel the sting of the thorns on each and every rose
Terrifying but normal

Eventually, they all recede to the wall again
Flattened as tissue, wallpaper and glue
Me in an empty room
Just imaginary memories of the world coming alive, but still
covered in scratches from rose thorns...


1/1/2020

*Photography by Johnny Perkins*

Apparitions

You were the ghost that was chasing me for years
But you were not transparent, like so many after you
You were solid white and opaque, like a bedsheet costume
Not able to see through you and to you, to your soul

But in the end your costume was tattered with loosened white
threads
You were just moments
You were only heartache
It would teeter between treating me like love and treating me like
an enemy
And that was never fair

Now you are just a faded ghost in my memory
Now you are transparent

The bedsheet tossed to the floor, stained and weathered
Your façade fallen and the shell of who you were remains haunting
me never again…

11/27/2019

The Owl


Toss to turn, tumbling, as done
Had a dream last night
Remembering owls and a friend who passed
For a moment, I thought it was you
Not letting tears flow
There was a sense of peace

The wingspan of the largest owl
Backdrops my view
Now seeing it is not you, any of you
It is the death of who we used to be
The end of me being the one used or abused

The owl wraps me in her wings
Comforts my loss
Then flies away, letting me be born as she releases me
Perhaps tonight dreams again, with fresh eyes, a fresh soul
And a single forgotten owl feather...


12/3/2019

Discarding

My soul laid horizontal for years letting one demon after another
have me and their faces changed some as my tears dried dirty on
my cheeks

Just resigned to be a rag doll used only when needed
For coins, entertainment, or sympathy
Then tossed in a pile until my time came up again
My dress grew stained dark and torn over years

But careful stitching to each arm and leg repaired me
Working so hard to regain all my stuffing again

Revealing my limbs broken but stitched, dirty but now brushed
clean, and well-worn but ready to be well loved

Always felt discarded each and every time, but truth be told, most
times, it was me who discarded them

The vicious the diablos that sought to cling to my pinafore dress
cannot gain their grip now that my button eyes can see their true
faces

Lost never finding, broken and unfixable, evil in pathetics

Brushing the dust off my dress and screwing in my new eyes, now
seeing the truth of the world beyond the buttons and torn stitches

You will haunt me well forever, but never again make me tear or
bleed viciously...


10/10/2020

Remember to Blink

You lulled me into an acceptable sense of nothingness
It was those wicked brown eyes you screwed in

You guided me like a child without the ability to see
Straight through the gates of hell and back

The soles of my feet burned yet without pain anymore
On that journey my hands plucked in new eyeballs too

You seem perplexed while my feet step backwards
Not realizing now my greens see your skeleton no heart no soul

Starting a new relationship on the ashes of an old one sounds quite
intriguing...


10/13/2020

*Photography by Johnny Perkins*

*Photography by Johnny Perkins*

Stained Impressions

The echo of you is all that remains, and you taste like iron and
sadness

In my memories though, we walk through cemeteries
Leave the rice paper and charcoal in the car and forget to do grave
rubbings

We just take pictures of the earthen homes of those who have died,
but relish the safety of graves
Not knowing more ways to die each day with the death around, our
love's death

The sweet smell of jasmine, the sun having stained the headstones
with the impression of our faces

But no time no space will ever fully wash away the sensation of
my fingertips on your rough skin
It only seeks to dull it; numbness and electricity collide
Infinite minute sources of energy form

We can create life, we have not yet mastered death...


7/24/2020

*Photography by Johnny Perkins*

## Shameful Dark

Darkness is where my beautiful hides in the dull deep shades and low light
Survival takes great strength and to thrive in this replica of damnation with demons for years

Having paid in all my blood already, now being able to claw my way out
Dirt under my fingernails, scratches on my arms, and red drips that circle my wrist

But freedom from this place is possible for me since shedding the faces behind the masks
Dirt washes clean eventually and eyes refocus on bits of small light that carry me further than thought of without my darkness

Not everything done in the dark is shameful...

4/26/2020

## Metal Handcuffs on Concrete

Quite many of my lovers have been destroyed when dreamt of
Curious passions of clumsy hands or ones bruising shoulder blades

Blissful daydreams that witched into nightmares like slow drip poison
Wondering just when it started to invade you and change even a cell

Tethering you to bad moments too long, handcuffed to dead lovers
Wrists cut and screaming red bleeding until you wither them free

What narrative scripts which exit next? With vicious words or rising shoulders
Having tasted curious passions and dragged the corpse of a dead lover

Scars left on my wrist scribbled red ink and wiped memories
What is left of my dead lovers clangs behind me, metal on concrete...

1/20/2021

*Photography by Johnny Perkins*

# My Philosophers

*It Isn't Manners by © Amy Kollar Anderson*
*Acrylic and glitter on canvas: 16" x 20" 2013 in private collection*

## Clean the Attic

Wherever you believe your soul comes from or goes
We all end up as ghosts haunting wood rafters

Caught in the spaces we used to reside
Tied up string tight to old photos of lost faces

In the interim though, with a broom we will go
Upstairs and clean out the cobwebs in the attic

Brushing away for many years or just for one day
Those old stale scents and memories that get in the way...


10/21/2020

## My Colors, My Hues

That precious yellow and green box of 96 colored wax sticks
wrapped in paper that we all received as children
How we looked forward to having a new box with a working
sharpener and razor points for that brief moment

The royal rare blues, the bleeding reds, the piercing sun of the
yellows, and the intoxicating purples
The beauty, the yearning, the tragedy, the disappointment, the
lessons, and the loss

But still, we color in shapes we know and shapes we do not yet
understand, in figures and images that trick our feelings
Now scratching heavily in color, screaming in color, and
screaming in moments on paper that will one day be read

Choosing to live deliberately, sketch deliberately, gather the curls
of sharpened colors that we never threw away deliberately
With life injected back into us, my cheeks full and blush red, my
light flickered back on, my dress on fire...

2/11/2020

*What She Was by Alberto Aprea*

## The Good Shelf

My memories are peppered with love and sit on the shelf with the
good crystal and knick-knacks
The figments of who we were in youth, longing to tell their stories,
words and whispers

Loves and sorrows, grave losses and triumphs, bad days and blurry
nights, half my memories are yours
Pouring out my stories on shelves and pages some white and more
curled and tear-stained

In the end will we fill pages with intoxicating adventures and
warm rainy days or maybe the paper will curl and wither in the
humid air?
Will the shelf hold more memories we cherish instead of detest?

While struggling to breathe, please give me breath
There are more stories to tell from these lips left parted...


6/25/2020

Galaxy


You left everyone behind as your metal and four wheels pulled away, no goodbyes
Never a soul or a face or part of a love retained
It was if they only existed in a handful of unviewed photos in an old stained box

But she, she was different than you and clung to people who impacted her life like a bomb
Several or many people knew masks she wore quite well
You knew the her that hid scared behind it and from it, you never ran

You always waxed the most silken of words and woven threads to her
When there was no one and nothing, you never left her behind, just tucked into your pocket saved her for when?

Each fairytale is really a nightmare if you read carefully
The witch is always destroyed, but is that her?
What if she is cleaver, kind, lovely, and just left of pretty?

Would you gravitate towards her with the same intensity of the planets as you do now?
In a lack of gravity could you still breathe someone in?

Spit out tiny comets and worlds only she will ever understand, because she was the one who remained...


7/21/2020

Blossoming

Fancying myself a painter that only painted flowers
Something about the birth of the petals that glow for a few days,
then drop down and perish

Opening to the world, for a brief moment and then dying
Fallen petal by fallen petal until the skeleton is revealed and
escaping...

2/12/2020

*Photography by Johnny Perkins*

*Photography by Johnny Perkins*

Tulip Leaves

Sometimes after whining about too much wine
My lips tell you stories that sit on the back shelf

Cautiously curious and always rather ridiculous they are
Some days of simple things and others wild adventures

You drink in my words like Moscato with tulip leaves
Mixing my words with a long metal spoon and something all too
sweet

Every time you let me recite a sonnet you feed that me that lives
just beneath my skin
Through veins and cells sucking in every intoxication to nourish
me

Leaving empty glasses once full of worlds of stories and wilted
tulip leaves...


8/9/2020

*Photography by Johnny Perkins*

Vanquish

Half the sounds that exit my lips are meant and said to you
Exhaled out with such purpose or dragon's breath
You occupy minutes or years inside my cerebellum

When silent, it is silence, just the beat of winged creatures and you
are missed
Your words are fiery and salted with lovely syllables
They burn the dragon's wings and sometimes mine too

But you are very far away to reach physically and my claws are
breaking reaching
They will heal eventually, as will my wings
So drown me wet in your language, your letters, your nouns

Make me see me like you do, speak to me as if we have no words
or eyes to focus
Taming the scaled fury back and resting my bloody claws in a
universe of blind love...


8/5/2020

*Photography by Johnny Perkins*

## Tea Party

My fingertips touch the surface of the mirror and it tactiles like water
Having to hold my breath just to dive back inside of it

The last few times tumbling down the rabbit hole, scuffing my knees, they bled
Each trip stains my dress with dirt and lands me hard on the ground below

It is a strange new world always, but it is the spinning universe of my mind
It draws me back in crazy and madly each and every time looking for you

Brushing off dust and dirt making my way through the trees
It always makes me question more, but I return still

Finding you where you haunt between the evergreens and your tea party, waiting for me
Trust me "I am mad about you hatter" and will keep accepting your invitations

Roses and queens be damned, for the creatures that live in here are never quite boring are they?

Hand me some tea and I will kiss the cup with my red lips
Left parted for your madness to seep in...


7/12/2020

*Photography by Johnny Perkins*

Bewitched

Inside my body, my entrails, my gut-wrenching soul
Live stories that will never be told loudly to strangers
Through some witchery, you enchant me enough to speak and only
you keep my deepest secrets

We have lived similarly tortured yet separate lives
Gravitating together somehow always like planets and stars with
gravity

Trick me with your sweet words? Your love? Let it bleed all over
me, I believe it
Peppering me with promises of delivered love and these syllables
that do not cut me, but protect me still

Through tricks or words mumble, you make sense to my cracked
insides and mind
Coming with yarn you sew through each piece of my broken heart

My soul has always found you in each and every lifetime
To restart my red beating when your words move me to insanity...

6/14/2020

Shimmer

Waxing and waning the truths of what we feel we deserve
Red moons, love that ignites the electricity in your skin
Tears that only run out of joy and gratefulness
It completely takes the breathe out of your lungs

Like the intricate mixing of many colors of storied glitter
Tiny moments that are forever entwined together
Because nothing good can be just separated like so
It would take a million years and equal seconds to pick each speck
apart

That is the entanglement of love or how we all hope and dream it
should be
Not the falls taken along the road, the way home, the dirt

Each fallen scraped knee, each tear, each drop of blood is a lesson
we had to learn
To better walk forward and collect new specks of glittered stories
until my pockets are full...


5/24/2020

*Photography by Johnny Perkins*

Honeybees

You have always recited the most honey of words
Tricking me beautiful like the nectar of the blooms they feed on

Making me flower each time you whisper the softest of syllables in
my ear
How we are together alone, that connection that no one else knows
nor understands

Will see you under the bright lights and neon, the sound of coins
and glasses clicking
To stop time and see if honey truly never spoils and no matter how
old we get, we still risk getting stung...

4/28/2020

*There Are Always Thorns by Alberto Aprea*

*Photography by Johnny Perkins*

## Spiral Staircase

Often times my soul spins downward, closer to the spiral staircase
end, days like today when all of my mad inside seems to come out
to play

As the circular spinning narrows on me, it allows out my darkest
and deepest, it seeps through and exposes exponentially strange
bits and pieces

But there you sit and the bottom of that impossibly large walk of
my memories filled with years of debris from tragic, but glittered
baubles, still left waiting

Hands out to catch the refined little bits of maybe my soul left
behind and cradle me in your arms in a circle
Halting the spiraling down and helping me learn to climb stair by
stair again until my soles bleed insanity…


7/15/2020

Memory Glass

Many half-full and desperately loved memories of blurry days and
moonlit nights
The joys of life, the broken hearts, the dizzy heads, and places we
should not have been

So many it is hard to carry them alone, like an enormous
collections of marbles
Each glass orb inspiringly unique in rich color and it's spinning
intricacies

But they are all mine still, the delightful and the obscure, each
good or bad dream
The spirit breaking and soul hitting wounds that roll between my
fingers

At times it can be quite a lot to carry, but they belong to me alone
and that is lovely and awful too
These beautiful pieces of glass burdened by my memories...


5/26/2020

*Photography by Johnny Perkins*

Storm Clouds

Always having loved in chaos
The brilliance of the storm as it swoops me in
Spins me, soaks me, runs electricity through me
It shocks me alive from the shallows of the dirt
Breath forced into my lungs, reviving me

But with that life comes another sort of death
That cannot be scraped off your skin, it is a disease
That taunts and tortures me until it rains again
But this downpour now fights to free me
When taking breathes in deeply

Being done with chaos, with storms
Choosing calm, temperate, pleasing weather now
As chaos is turbulent and frigid
Not desiring a weatherman nor a storm chaser

Love is the storm once not controlled by me
It just spun me dizzy intoxicated, but now
Lightening tickles through my veins and seethes chaos
To love in the center of the tornado, where it is still and silent, and
safe from the ravage of swift vicious winds…

1/6/2020

Lost Luggage


Pushed to the breaking point with demands
Makes me want to take time off from drama
Or trauma or whatever choosing to call my past
Loving being alone, eating alone, falling in love with an idea alone
is extraordinarily exciting now

Striving now for many stamps on my passport
Finding myself lost in places never been
Thriving now filled with tulips not death root growing
Therefore, alone with myself is priceless and lovely

The dents in my luggage will be the only bruises carried from now
on down cobblestone streets where dreams grow
Be wisdom without regret of the past
Always moving towards future sunsets…


12/27/2019

*Photography by Johnny Perkins*

## Pretty but Crazy

She paints on her eyes with dark lines and black mascara, thinking it hides her tears if they fall silently behind

Well lived and lived over many rough long days and sleepless nights, well educated, but dumb with love and broken promises

Daydreaming of finding a soul that understands her insides and of butterflies and flowers melting in her hands

She waxes on the nostalgic and wants to learn to love rightly, as she is lovely sometimes with words and pretty but crazy...

7/19/2020

*Photography by Johnny Perkins*
*Art Rag Doll by Heather Dittmar*

Fearlessly


That strange feeling after being left and discarded
Gutted from the inside where everything is stolen

As if every organ, every bone, every blood vessel has been
removed
Your skin holding the shape of who you used to be

Wind whistling through empty hollow cavities
Places where my heart and lungs and soul used to live

The torturous years that followed holding up that body of skin
Slowly filling the emptiness with bits of light

Until finally my bones have grown themselves in
My veins have risen connected and pulsed red

My breath had kept me seeming full, but now it is real
My arms and legs can move to reach, run, and love fearlessly...


10/10/2020

*Photography by Johnny Perkins*

Phoenix

My mind she tells stories constantly, some out loud and some
screamed within
Stories of forevers and always, stories with words that drip like
rain off the windowsill

Words that encircle me for there exists no mathematical equation
that exists to equal love

There is no card drawn, whether queen or joker that tells the future
of love

What we dream upon maybe is unrealistic or just overrated
But dreams of love, they seep in still, from the deepest part of my
mind

There should not be days or words we cannot navigate through
when entwined with love
That if you study any work of art up close, you will see each and
every mistake

The dramatic end, the crash, the burn, the phoenix rising from the
ashes of death and blossoming into a fiery orange red everything...

7/20/2020

J 'adore la Danse

Walking the stage mark, the fine line of average and crazy in pale
pink pointe shoes
She chose ballet and tulle costumes over athletic pursuits

Most days she draped typical, but spoke strange enough to be
noticed
She was not quite normal like a cutter split cookie, but she was
extraordinary

After years of walking in uncomfortable shoes, she slipped quietly
into her own skin again
The slightly left of center became endearing and once more words
bled through lovely

Her journey into splendid, the soul touched just underneath the
skin
It bleeds out with a blade's kiss and she knows whenever
something doesn't go right, tomorrow something will...


8/18/2020

*Dance Me Hilariously Insane by Alberto Aprea*

*Photography by Johnny Perkins*

## Pages of Poison

We all have parts that scare us, so we hide them deep within, but
never well enough, no costume covers
Those loves and thoughts and poisoned memories that scarred us
inside but left the outside unbruised

The well-lived stories you never wanted to read again, curled leaf
and the smell of old pages turning
In time we all need to dive into the book and let the poison of the
watered-down memories envelope us

For everything we wear is a costume though, isn't it?
Just peeling away layer after layer to see to the next
Eventually, getting to those hard to read and hard to understand
novels of you

It is impossible to hide from who we truly are and then again, why
would we want to?
You love my bittersweet stories and drink them in volumes and
long to read every inch and bruise of me

Hate is inches from love and you are my kind of poison...


4/26/2020

*Photography by Johnny Perkins*
*Art Rag Doll by Heather Dittmar*

Bath Water

You still rest your old tired heart on your tattered sleeve
It bleeds into the fabric staining the threads a deep red

My anger when she is awoken is resting on my sleeve with
branches
Unable to trick unbothered, my thoughts spit like raindrops from
my lips

You exhale out the most honey of words to me each time you
breathe me in
You broke me first, but that was a nightmare quite a lifetime ago

My black rose of a silent voice now screams loudly when scared to
speak
The part that most shocks me shakes me still and now my lips
move

Thankfully with some witchery of fate, you soak in my words like
bath water
Soothe my aching heart and still the tricksters that clip to my
sleeves...

9/4/2020

## Umbrellas on a Rock

Conjured the words near water to get it all out in volumes
The rocks and shore where my screams were not silenced

Finding out after all of the venom seeps out, there exists
Beautiful syllables exposing our truths and lured fictions

Philosophers be damned and listen to memories re-crafted
Just my broken stories wrapped tight in black ribbons

Once expelled from my scarred throat it cleanses me
Discarding the photograph in my head that was horrifying

Sitting outside scripting sonnets, worms crawl in my head
Holding an umbrella just to block the rain and more worms
sneaking in...


9/17/2020

## Pied-à-terre

Easy to find, but very hard to know
My eyes are always open wide, green, and listening
But never seeing the truth of the ugliness before me

For over a dozen years the walls were silent
Living a life without any music or sound
Paint that breathed dry and never exhaled

Quiet breeds quite complacency
Seeking only the truth now through crickets
Along the bank of our secret pied-à-terre

Nestled safe in our own honesty
You spit words so lovely with each pant
Opening my hearing, vision, and heart still grieving...


9/27/2020

*Photography by Johnny Perkins*
*Art Rag Doll by Heather Dittmar*

## Rag Doll

When it comes down to the reality of it, my skin's not porcelain
Simply a doll with not much my hands can offer
They do not work and hang on wires with empty mittens

Just my heart sewn inside my stuffing with thread and patches
Resigned to the corner shelf with old photos and bad dreams
Remembering my usefulness from quite long ago

Paint me pretty again, green-eyed, and not so dusty
Clean my tea-stained dress bleached back fresh white
Set me on the good shelf where the postcards are kept

Mailed from adventures we have yet to live loudly
Lands my tired feet will reach as you set me down gently
Not caring if my lace looks worn or my face has small cracks

Your words still sing lovely like honey bees or glue
To hold my stitches together with sweet lips and kindness

Your broom sweeping by the last cobweb that remains
What is left is a heart once discarded in pain
Tap on some glue and try to pretend, this once pretty doll is
beautiful again...

10/2/2020

*Photography by Johnny Perkins*

## Raised Red Memories

Pretending that cut never existed does not make it go away in the wind
It always blows back hard with a sharp breeze and a stolen kiss

Escaping the chains, the ropes, the threads requires quite sharp knives
That steal bits of your blood as they slip ripping across the binding

But worthy of the escape through veins or bruises, so we are taught
Etch lessons in our skin over time and they loudly tell our stories

Some are wicked and some damning and some not worth repeating
But the fingerprints of scars still trail along our bodies

Mapping the worlds, our oceans, our giant timber and bad memories
Trace me with rough callused fingers and years of aching wisdom...

10/1/2020

*Photography by Johnny Perkins*

Habitually focused on how your irises focus in on me critically examining
My reflection in your eyes and mirror is never what is desired and it disappoints

Spent too many hours and years chasing down pretty for what purpose?
Never feeling her caught, just resolving to resting in the normal space of life

Painting on color and loving every prettying moment but still somewhat crooked inside
That is me wrapped tight in a big black bow with eyes that speak trickery but never trick

Never now resigning to drowning in your tea cup of boiling hot leaves and water
My sights are set mesmerized on the your big irises and my reflection in your sights...

9/1/2020

*Photography by Johnny Perkins*

## Like Shards of Glass


Your blood whines screeching from your lips
The singular sounds heard in the garden dark
Reviving me quite after over a decade of sleeping

Wherever my soul had been resting uncomfortably
You plucked me up and put me back inside
That empty shell that walked barefoot was me

Loose in my skin again with tendons and muscles
Screwing in my eyeballs to make me see
Unsewing my quieted lips to learn to speak up

Shaking off the last bits of old dust and debris
That demons left on this once empty shell
Filling my heart red with blood and soul shards...


10/4/2020

In Good Spirits

Horror stories that creep into your life over time
Things that would terrify quite most others
You have been down those paths no one picks too

Sometimes with me and sometimes without me there
But we carry bushels of rocks together and alone
Always forced to be the savior despite the consequences

It seems easier with four hands, but two are ghostly
Waiting impatiently for them to grow in skin and bones
Slipping your fingertips between mine fusing apparition

Tying together secret messages on our wrists
Spoken in a language only we speak fluently
Telling each other millions of stories with just the touch of our
skin...


10/27/2020

*Photography by Johnny Perkins*

*Photography by Johnny Perkins*

## Pied Piper

My monocle raised to my newly screwed in eye
Viewing my life through the lens of creativity

Language to me is like the breath or sex face
That we have all made lost in the illusion of creating

It hums in the distance always looming and intoxicating
Like a rat following the flute song

Bathe me in your artwork with sharp brushstrokes
Paint my bare skin in colors that turn into words aching...


11/18/2020

*Photography by Johnny Perkins*
*Graphic Design by Marie Lee*

## Beautiful but Damaged

Using always only big words, expensive ones, sentences full of
adjectives and verbs
The language of letters that can string together in such beauty is
astonishing

Her stories sound like catastrophes, but they were all needed and
well-earned lessons
Life is a long time to feel foolish or dumb, so choosing not to is an
easy decision

But weeks or months to years is also a long time to feel anything
but beautiful as she has
She sees pretty in the mirror now because you tell her to each day

Attempting to paint a true picture of just which train she got onto,
is it truth or lies
Asking others to make sure he had not taught her to trick herself
beautiful

But she sees the scars remain too, reminders that she is beautiful
but damaged...


8/1/2020

*Photography by Johnny Perkins*

Pocketworms


Wondering if the wishing well is filled with poison
Hold my hand tight and still jump in with me

Carry an umbrella as my words drip over you like honey
Let yourself drown in it quite silly would you

Trace our road with your fingertip on a map and photograph
Make me adore the journey with just you more each moon

My throat wet still with sips of well water with worms
Licking the dirt of nature off my lips

Each poisonous kiss tastes like the bees made it
Run with me down the road, dirt on my dress, and worms stealing
rides in my pockets...


9/8/2020

*Photography by Johnny Perkins*

Enchant Me

There seems to be some witchery spinning concentric circles
around my finger keys

Galaxies of wisdom within my cells that spark bright that
somewhat entrances me light

Which part of me was it that deliciously just transforms you into
everything?

Each time feeling having failed a thing with disappointment or
fears to bring

Your words wipe my tears and alleviate my fears that little things
are pebbles not Everest

Remarkable seems like it hums quite right or echoes all my
thoughts just right

Though thank yous make you cringe sigh and say it does not have
magick that way

Still things are cast most weeks or days and some spells just work
out one day...


11/8/2020

#fearless


Comfortable being uncomfortable for most of my life
Stuffed full of cotton and stitched every thread up so tight

Patchwork pinafore dress on with years of dirt stains
Profoundly tired of all this, my pinned heart refrains

Discarded me? Sure there have been a few times
Mostly though there is a secret my heart leaves behind

That my black shell well-crafted each theatrical show
Each orchestrated leaving my laughter quite flowed

It is time to be comfortable in dresses and flats
Frankly, anything that makes me feel pretty like that

Discard my old dress and unpin my healed heart
Never again let anyone try to tear it apart

Been told "you're a doll" as an old friend would say
Wiping off the last dirt and heading off in the away...


12/16/2020

*Photography by Johnny Perkins*

*Now Go Paint Your Own Roses by Alberto Aprea*

# THE END

*for today...*

# ARTIST
# CONTIBUTORS

An immense thank you to the five talented artists that joined this novel-in-poems journey with me. My vision would not be a reality without their beautiful visual storytelling contributions. Take a moment to learn about each exceptional artist on the following pages. "Remember to thank those who inspire you"

*Kaytee*

# Artist Contributor

## Alberto Aprea
### *Fine Artist, Argentina*

*Photography by Santiago Aprea*

**Visit the links below to learn more about this talented artist
who joined my romantically macabre journey**

https://www.instagram.com/apreaalberto/

https://albertoaprea.artstation.com/
https://www.youtube.com/c/DrawTaller

**Thank you Alberto…**

# Artist Contributor

## Johnny Perkins
### *Photographer, United States*

*Photography by Johnny Perkins*

**Visit the links below to learn more about this talented artist who joined my romantically macabre journey**

https://www.green-lion-studios.com/

https://linktr.ee/greenlionstudios

**Thank you Johnny…**

# Artist Contributor

## Amy Kollar Anderson
### *Fine Artist, United States*

*Photography by Mark Anderson*

**Visit the links below to learn more about this talented artist
who joined my romantically macabre journey**

**http://www.kollaranderson.com/**

**https://www.instagram.com/amykollaranderson/**

**Thank you Amy…**

# Artist Contributor

## Friederike Gröpler
### *Fine Artist, Germany*

*Photography by Jessica Körber*

**Visit the links below to learn more about this talented artist
who joined my romantically macabre journey**

https://www.instagram.com/fryda.gorgon.art/

https://www.patreon.com/FrydaGorgonArt
https://www.etsy.com/de/shop/frydagorgonart
https://www.artstation.com/frydagorgonart

**Thank you Friederike…**

# Artist Contributor

## Heather Dittmar
### *Doll Artist, United States*

*Photography by Heather Dittmar*

**Visit the link below to learn more about this talented artist who joined my romantically macabre journey**

https://heartfeltplush.com/links

**Thank you Heather…**

# Artist Credits – Official Logo Design

**Glass Half Full Goth logo**
*Glass Half Full Goth by Alberto Aprea*
*Graphic Design by Marie Lee*
**#glasshalffullgoth**

**October City Press logo**
*Squash from the Witness series by Fryda Gorgon Art by Friederike Gröpler*
*Graphic Design by Marie Lee*
**#octobercitypress**

Pause

Until next time
Words trickle off the edge of the page
My hands outstretch to catch each letter as it falls
Filling my pockets with future stories
To be unfolded and told next time…

7/28/2022

CPSIA information can be obtained
at www.ICGtesting.com
Printed in the USA
BVHW060208021122
650792BV00003B/8